My Mother Always Used to Say

My Mother Always Used to Say

Valerie Bowe

LONDUBH BOOKS

First published in 2010 by Londubh Books
18 Casimir Avenue, Harold's Cross, Dublin 6w
www.londubh.ie
3 5 4 2
Cover by bluett; origination by Londubh Books
Printed in Ireland by ColourBooks, Baldoyle Industrial Estate, Dublin 13
ISBN: 978-1-907535-05-5
The author has asserted her moral rights.
Copyright © The Contributors
Introduction © Valerie Bowe 2009

The proceeds of this book will go to the Kitty Whittle Fund, which will be administered by Lourdes Youth and Community Services (LYCS), Sean McDermott Street, Dublin 1, to provide education bursaries for lone parents.

This book is dedicated to all the contributors who have so generously donated what their mother/father/grandparents used to say. Without them this book could not have been published. It is also dedicated to my mother, Kitty Whittle, who used to say, 'Never tell your husband how much you paid for a dress.'

Contents

Acknowledgements 11
Introduction to 2010 Edition 15
Introduction 17
Contributors 23-159

Acknowledgements

I am indebted to Alison McNamara, who during the summer of 2008, helped me to forage for the contact details of celebrities. I am very grateful to Jo O'Donoghue, Publisher, Londubh Books, who believed in this book from the moment I presented it to her, to graphic artist, Syd Bluett, for his wonderful cover and bookmark, and to all those involved in the sale and distribution of the first three printings.

Thanks to all my friends and family who knew somebody who knew somebody who knew a celebrity, in particular to Sarah Cronin and Lee Sim who exhausted their contact books and to Katy McAndrew, who is a good friend and told me to stop talking about the book and just do it.

Thanks to Rena Stokes in Tramore, who was there every step of the way and rang people up and convinced them it was a good idea to contribute; to author Finn

Mac Eoin who lives in Provence and to whom all the French contributions – and more – can be attributed; to Fergus Forde who hand-delivered a letter to a celebrity he knew, something that had a very fruitful response; to Dave Fennell who offered to invest in this project, if needed, so convinced was he of its merits and future success and whom I named 'My First Dragon'; to Helena McNeill for her unfailing encouragement and for being an amazing person and an ambassador for development education; to Mickey McCormick for mining his contact book and coming up trumps; to my cousin, Rhoda Cunningham, who was very generous with her support; to George Hunter, who kept Alison and myself in lovely fresh scones and gave us a few laughs over the summer of 2008; to Mary McCann and Geraldine Toner who are great people and have great contacts too; to Helena Browner, Christine Kelly, Jackie Towers, Molly O'Duffy, Pauline Bergin, Sally McEllistrim and Suzanne O'Coineen for all their support and friendship.

Thanks to all in Lourdes Youth and Community Services where I worked for four very happy years, in particular to director Sarah Kelleher who is a source of inspiration and who heads an organisation that does Trojan work in the area of community education;

to chairperson, John Farrelly, and treasurer, Celsus Fennell. The administration of the proceeds of this book will be entrusted into the safe hands of these three individuals.

Thanks to my beloved son, Nicholas, for all the chats about the book and the long philosophical conversations about life and who recently surprised himself by repeating to his daughter my saying: 'The man who wins is the man who thinks he can.' Thanks also to my adorable six-year-old granddaughter who one day placed her elbows on the kitchen table and rested her head in her hands, looked thoughtfully at me and said: 'Do you know, Nana Val, that your heart is your brain, and your brain – it's just your brain.' Wise woman, Saoirse!

Not everyone I got in touch with was in a position to contribute to the book, and I would like to extend my thanks to those who sent correspondence and good wishes in response to my letter:

President Mary McAleese; President Horst Koehler of Germany; President Vaclav Klaus of the Czech Republic; Her Majesty Queen Margrethe II of Denmark; Her Majesty Queen Beatrix of the Netherlands; HSH Prince Albert II of Monaco; President Tarja Halonen of the Republic of Finland;

Prime Minister Helen Clarke of New Zealand; HRH The Prince of Wales; HRH The Duke of Edinburgh; HRH The Duke of York; Her Majesty Queen Elizabeth II; Doris Day; Arsène Wenger; Michael Flatley; Graham Norton; Bob Geldof; Bill Gates.

Thank you all.

Introduction to the 2010 Edition

I was amazed by the reaction of the media and the public to the publication of the first edition of *My Mother Always Used to Say* in October 2009. The book was reprinted twice within six weeks and still managed to sell out before Christmas. The demand has been so great that this new expanded edition is being published for Mother's Day in March 2010. Again all the proceeds from the book will go to the Kitty Whittle Fund which will provide education bursaries for lone parents. This fund is being administrated by Lourdes Youth and Community Services, Sean McDermott Street, Dublin 1.

I would like to take this opportunity to thank everyone who bought a copy of the book and also say thanks to the media who took the book to their hearts and so kindly wrote about it and covered it on radio and television. I had great fun hearing all the sayings from Donegal right down to Waterford when listeners and viewers rang in to shows with what their mothers always used to say. The response was huge because at the end of the day we are all sons and daughters, whether we are celebrities or not.

Next Christmas the new edition of the book will contain mostly sayings from readers. Maybe your mother had a unique way of saying things. If so I would love to hear from you. Sayings that are a bit out of the ordinary will have a better chance of being in the book. While the book is entitled *My Mother Always Used To Say*, you are also very welcome to contribute sayings handed down by fathers/grandparents/guardians – anyone who was near and dear to you when you were growing up. Everyone is invited to contribute to the Christmas 2010 edition.

Email me at valentinebowe@gmail.com or post your saying on www.mymotheralwaysusedtosay.ie.

I hope you enjoy this new expanded edition of *My Mother Always Used to Say* and hope that it might prompt you to look back with nostalgia at the sayings your mother/father/grand-parent emphasised in order to guide you through the world.

Valerie Bowe
February 2010

Introduction

The germ of the idea for this book first came to me when I was reading *An Evil Cradling,* that masterpiece by Brian Keenan. I remember a scene in that book in which, in order to help John McCarthy to move out of his distress, the author keeps repeating something John's mother used to say to his father. It left a lasting impression on me. It struck me then how very potent these repetitive sayings we hear in childhood are, and the lasting influence they have on us.

The seed was planted.

After that I began to notice that in practically every interview, in both the broadcast and print media, celebrities would recall what their parents said to them as children.

In my work as coordinator of Henrietta Adult and Community Education (HACE) Services I chatted to a number of the participants and they too recalled what their mother or father or grandparents used to say. I thought about my own parents and, lo and behold, I began to recall vividly what I had heard in childhood. I felt confident, then, that all families have this oral tradition that is succinctly gathered into phrases or sayings. In fact, our parents taught us through this oral wisdom.

When I worked in the area of community education, it was a revelation to me that you don't need to be able to read or write in order to be a teacher: that, regardless, of their literacy skills, all parents are teachers and this is a methodology.

When I was a child, one of my hobbies was collecting words of wisdom and pasting them into my scrapbook. My primary source was my mother's towering collection of past editions of *Woman's Weekly*. At the bottom of the problem page of this magazine, there were always two wise sayings. When my mother was finished with the magazines I would slice into the problem page and retrieve these two pearls of wisdom. Occasionally I would nudge myself to read the problems!

All these experiences merged and the idea for the book was born. I talked about the idea for two years or so, really because I didn't know how to go about it and was afraid to embark on such an adventure. Until a friend told me to stop talking about it and do it. Oh! *How* do you do that? Write to people and ask them!

I then decided to compile the book and donate the proceeds to a cause dear to my heart: women parenting alone. I became a single mother myself in the 1970s and am now a grandmother.

All the royalties from this book will go to a fund named after my own mother, the Kitty Whittle Fund, which will provide education bursaries for lone parents.

The journey has taken me a number of years to complete. After work in the evening I wrote a couple of letters and my shopping regularly included a book of stamps. Again, it became a hobby, like my hobby in childhood. No pressure: just enjoyment. I was giving it a go. I still didn't know if it would work but when Sir Alex Ferguson contributed I knew that the book was possible. Besides myself, there were others who were starting to believe in it. During a career break in the summer of 2008 I put my foot on the accelerator and broke the back of the book

While the book is called *My Mother Always Used to Say,* in the spirit of inclusiveness, contributors were asked to contribute sayings handed down by mothers or fathers, grandparents or guardians. But the majority contributed what their mother used to say.

How important are these repetitive sayings we hear in childhood? The animal kingdom has ably demonstrated what can happen without this method of learning. I was very interested to see on a television documentary that, as a result of the foot-and-mouth epidemic in England during which tens of thousands of sheep were put down, flock memory was lost and the young lambs kept falling off the mountain. They had no older sheep to guide them and pave the way. No intergenerational words (bah!) of wisdom.

I hope you enjoy the book and have some fun with it and above all that you look back with new interest at the words that your mother/father/grandparent uttered to guide you through the world.

Valerie Bowe, October 2009

Note: for readers unfamiliar with the title 'TD', it means *Teachta Dála*, a member of the Irish *Dáil* or parliament.

Gerry Adams, President, Sinn Fein

My mother always used to say, 'The least said, the soonest mended.'

Bertie Ahern TD, Former Taoiseach

Before I went out the door to play a match, my mother always used to say, 'Good God, tonight.'

Dermot Ahern TD, Minister for Justice, Equality and Law Reform

My mother always used to say, 'You cannot make a silk purse out of a sow's ear.'

I also remember my father saying: 'And they say there's no money in the country…'

Mohamed Al Fayed, Chairman, Harrods

My mother always used to say, 'Look after your brothers and sisters.'

Darina Allen,
Ballymaloe Cookery School

My mother's advice to mothers of younger children was, 'Keep your mouth shut and your door open.'

Another one was the recipe for good family relationships with your son-in-law and daughter-in-law: 'Don't voice an opinion unless you're asked for it and don't visit unless you are invited.'

Rachel Allen, Cook

My mother, Hallfridur O'Neill, always says, 'What will be will be.'

Barry Andrews TD, Minister for Children and Youth Affairs

My mother always used to say, 'When one door closes another door opens.'

Jeffrey Archer, Author

My mother always used to say, 'When you know you're beaten, give in gracefully.'

Brigitte Bardot, French Film Star and Founder, the Brigitte Bardot Foundation

Ma mēre a toujours dit, 'Bien faire et laisser braire.' (Do your best and don't pay any attention to the critics.)

Sean Barrett TD

My mother always used to say, 'Show me your friends and I'll tell you who you are.'
and
'The mind is like a parachute – it doesn't work unless it's open.'

Floella Benjamin OBE, Actress, Writer, Children's Campaigner and Chancellor of University of Exeter

My mum used to say, 'Education is your passport to life. Once you've got it no one can take it away from you.'

Laura Bermingham, Model and Journalist

My mother was able to cook mince in a huge variety of ways but I would rather have swallowed my own foot than eaten it. She used to make me sit there and she'd say, 'You are not moving until that plate is empty.'

She also used to tell me, 'Save a few bob because that modelling malarkey could just end suddenly one day.'

Pauline Bewick, Visual Artist

My mother always used to say, 'Listen to your body when eating.'

Maeve Binchy, Author

My mother and father always used to say that 'How are you?' is a greeting, not a question.

Frances Black,
Singer and Songwriter

My mother always used to say, 'What is seldom is wonderful.'
and
'A nod is as good as a wink to a blind horse.'

Cherie Blair QC

My grandma always said, 'If a job's worth doing, it's worth doing well,' and that's as true today as it was then.

Tony Blair,
Former UK Prime Minister

My mother always used to say, 'Don't let your eyes be bigger than your stomach.'

Neil Blaney TD

My mother always used to say, 'What's meant for you won't go by you.'

Dermot Bolger,
Author and Playwright

My father always used to say, 'Do anything you want with your life but just don't go to sea.'

Valerie Bowe, Author

My mother, Kitty Whittle, always used to say, 'Never tell your husband how much you paid for a dress.'

Tommy Bowe, Irish Rugby Team, British and Irish Lions

My mother is a great believer in the healing power of plenty of sleep and if there was ever anything wrong with you she would say, 'Get a big glass of water and some vitamins into you and get to bed and you'll wake up as right as rain – you'll be one hundred per cent.'

Olive Braiden,
Human Rights Commissioner

My mother always used to say, 'People have their own troubles; try not to add to them.'

Gay Byrne, Broadcaster

My mother always used to say, 'Prepare yourself, the opportunity will come.'

Mark Cagney, Host, *Ireland AM*

One of my father's favourites sayings was, 'Don't worry about being popular, worry about being good. Popular comes and goes; good always works.' He was a musician and he used to drum this into his music students.

Another saying of my father, although it undoubtedly came from his grandfather, a farmer from north Cork whose five sons went to university in the early part of the last century, was, 'Knowledge is no weight.'

The third saying I got from my aunt: '*Dum spiro spero*,' which is Latin for, 'While I breathe, I hope.' It is eternally optimistic and says you are never beaten. After my first wife died, this one was well and truly tested and it didn't fail me!

Pierre Cardin,
Fashion Designer

Ma mère a toujours dit, 'Regard toujours devant, jamais derrière.' (Always look forward, never backwards.)

Victoria Mary Clarke, Journalist

My mother, Orla, used to say, 'Children should be free to do whatever they want to do, whenever they want, and to express themselves; and children should be listened to carefully.'

My grandmother, Frances, used to say, 'Don't worry: you'll have forgotten about it by the time you are twenty-one.' I suppose when I got to twenty-one she must have extended it.

Bill Clinton, Former US President

'My mother:

It was she who taught me to get up every day and keep going;

To look for the best in people even when they saw the worst in me;

To be grateful for every day and greet it with a smile;

To believe I could do or be anything I put my mind to if I was willing to make the requisite effort;

To believe that, in the end, love and kindness would prevail over cruelty and selfishness.'

Michael Colgan, Artistic Director, the Gate Theatre

My mother always used to say, 'Marry for money and you'll earn it.'

Ronan Collins, Broadcaster

My mother always used to say, 'It's easy to say money doesn't matter when you have plenty of it.'

Eoghan Corry,
Journalist and Author

My mother, Anne Corry (1929-2009), used to say, 'Is iomaí lá sa chill orainn.' ('We're a long time in the graveyard.') She learned her Gaeilge growing up in Clahanmore in west Clare, eavesdropping on her grandparents, who used it as a *teanga rúnda*. Like many of the generation whose lifespan brought them from tilly lamps to mobile phones, she was a great woman in a crisis, and had a few to keep her on her toes: the death of dad in 1971, leaving her with four teenage children, the death of my niece Anne, who was stillborn, in 1986, and the accident that paralysed my brother in 1990. I thought of the phrase when we laid her to rest in Straffan churchyard, with the birds singing, in February 2009.

Emer Costello,
Lord Mayor of Dublin

My mother always used to say, 'If you can't say something nice, say nothing.'

Alan Cotton,
British Landscape Painter

When things went wrong, my mother would say, 'Ah well, worse things happen at sea.'

The words of wisdom she gave me when I had kids of my own were: 'The best gifts you can give your children are roots and wings.' She meant to give them the confidence to leave you and go out into the world and the assurance that they can always come back home.

Mary Coughlan TD, Tánaiste and Minister for Enterprise, Trade and Employment

My mother always used to say, 'You can't cook unless you're in the kitchen.'

Simon Coveney TD

My father always used to say, 'Never the backward glance – energy lost on worrying about the past is wasted energy.'

Una Crawford O'Brien, Actress, *Fair City*

My mother had two sayings: 'You'll be better before you're twice married,'

and

'Better to say, "There you are," than, "Where are you?"'

John Creedon, Broadcaster

My mother used to say, 'Banks will happily loan you an umbrella when the sun shines. As soon as it rains they ask for it back.'

Frank Crummey,
Activist and Author

My mother, Elizabeth, used to say, 'You know you're a genius and you can do anything you like in this world.'

Bill Cullen, Businessman and Irish Host of *The Apprentice*

My mother's mother, Molly Darcy, always used to say, 'Every day you can get out of bed is a great day.'

Peter Cunningham, Author and Journalist

My father always used to say, 'People who don't ask how much don't intend to pay.'

Chris de Burgh, Singer and Songwriter

My father always used to say to my brother and myself, 'If a thing is worth doing, it is worth doing well.' This has often been in my mind during my thirty-five years in the music business.

Noel Dempsey TD, Minister for Transport

My mother always used to say, 'You can't make an omelette without breaking eggs.'

Ian Dempsey, Broadcaster

My mother always used to say, 'Put a bit of Savlon on it,' (the universal cure)

and

'Always think of how the other person is feeling – not yourself,' (It's not all about you, y'know.)

and

'Eat that up big.' It started as, 'Eat that and you will grow up to be big,' but was shortened after she said it for the millionth time.

Lynsey Dolan,
Broadcaster, Country Mix

A favourite quote that came from my dad, who raised me, was, 'Never save something for a special occasion: every day in your life is a special occasion.'

Anne Doyle, Newscaster

My mother always used to say, 'Don't let your bone go with the dog.'
 and
'The sun will rise tomorrow.'

Damien Duff,
Republic of Ireland Footballer

My mother always used to say, 'There is light at the end of the tunnel.'

Gavin Duffy,
Entrepreneur, Serial Investor
and Dragon on *Dragon's Den*

My mother, Anne Duffy, always used to say, 'If it's for you it won't go by you.'

Joe Duffy, Broadcaster

My mother, Mabel, used to say, 'You are never better than anyone else or worse than anyone else.'

Paraic Duffy, Director General, GAA

My mother always used to say, 'Look after the pennies and the pounds will look after themselves.'

Kevin Dundon, Chef and Hotelier

My mother always used to say, 'Two wrongs are never right.'

Olwyn Enright TD

My mother always used to say, 'You'll eat, and you will like it.'

Bernard Farrell, Playwright

My mother always used to say, 'Never be turned by the flattering tongue,'
and
'Imagination keeps the crows flying.'
My father used to say, 'You can take a horse to the well but a pencil is always lead.'

Mairead Farrell, Broadcaster and TV Panellist

My mother always said, 'Never leave the house without make-up on: you never know who you are going to meet.

Sir Alex Ferguson CBE, Manager, Manchester United FC

My mother always used to say, 'Don't get too big for your boots.'

Colette Fitzpatrick, Newscaster, TV3

My mother always used to say, 'When the bills come in the letterbox, love goes out the window.'

Frank Flannery,
Director of Organisation, Fine Gael

My mother was a woman of strong convictions, who did not change her mind easily, so we often heard when we wanted something new: 'That would be the last stone in my beads.'

Tony Flannery, Priest and Writer

My mother never believed in borrowing or getting into debt. Her expression for this was, 'Never eat tomorrow's dinner today.'

Beverley Flynn TD

My mother always used to say, 'All the flowers of our tomorrows are in the seeds of today,'
   and
   'Laugh and the world laughs with you: weep and you weep alone.'

Quentin Fottrell, Author and Journalist

My mother, Pauline Fottrell, says, 'It doesn't matter if you're gay, straight or ambidextrous!'

CORNELIA FRANCES,
ACTRESS, *HOME AND AWAY*

My mother always used to say, 'Always be yourself – and always take a safety pin when you go out.'

Finbar Furey, Singer

My father always used to say, 'If you can be yourself for at least one-third of your life, you'll always win.'

Sorcha Furlong, Actress, *Fair City*

My mother used to say to me, 'What's for you, won't pass you.'

PJ Gallagher, *Naked Camera*

The one thing my mother always used to say, and still does, is, 'Prevention is better than cure.'

Diarmuid Gavin, Garden Designer and TV Presenter

My mother always used to say, 'Your mother's never wrong.'

Eamon Gilmore TD, Leader, the Labour Party

My mother always used to say, 'God never closes one door without opening another.'

Larry Gogan, Broadcaster

My mother always used to say, 'Take care of the pennies and the pounds will take care of themselves.'

John Gormley TD, Minister for the Environment and Leader, Green Party

My father always used to say, 'If you want to do a job, do it yourself.'

Tony Gregory (1947-2009)
TD, Dublin Central

My mother always used to say, 'Your health is your wealth and your friend is your pocket.'

Hugo Hamilton, Author

My mother always used to say, 'If you bake in anger, it will taste of doubt and you will make an unhappy cake.'

Mary Harney,
Minister for Health and Children

My mother always used to say, 'Never forget where you came from.'

Ainsley Harriott,
Star of *Ready, Steady, Cook*

Mum used to say, 'A new broom sweeps clean but an old broom knows the corners.'

Sean Haughey TD

My father always used to say, 'There is no one from whom you cannot learn something.'

Seamus Heaney,
Poet and 1995 Nobel Laureate

My mother always used to quote a neighbour of ours, a Scotch woman whose accent she was also very fond of imitating, 'It's no' the things you bargain for, Mrs Heaney, it's the things that crop up.'

Fiona Hoban,
Psychotherapist and Author

My mother, Mary, used to say, 'Never trouble trouble until trouble troubles you. For if you trouble trouble, trouble will trouble you.'

Tom Hopkins, Actor, *Fair City*

Mam was full of sayings which my father referred to as 'pishoges' (a gentle reminder to her that she was from the 'wesht' while he was a dyed-in-the-wool Dub. His parents were both from beyond the Pale!)

Mostly these were of the, 'Never walk under a ladder,' and, 'Green is for grief' variety.

Also, she used to say, 'We've seen the two days,' and, 'Idle hands are the devil's workshop.'

My Roscommon grandmother, a mother of ten, was often heard to bemoan: 'Guinness! There's a baby in every bottle.'

Gloria Hunniford,
the Caron Keating Foundation

My mother always said, 'In life you should always have a really good bed and a really good pair of shoes, because you are either in one or the other.'

Jenny Huston,
DJ and Radio Broadcaster

My mother, Jane, always used to say, 'If you can't be good, be careful,' as I was heading out the door as a teenager.

Kate Hyde, Founder of Henparty.ie and Participant in *Dragon's Den*

My mother, Verna Whyte, always used to say, 'Listen to all but follow your own instincts.'

Jeremy Irons, Actor

My mother always used to say, 'It takes all sorts to make a world.'

Jennifer Johnston, Author

My mother always used to say, 'It takes two to tango.'

Gerald Kean, Solicitor and Author

My mother used to say, 'Always remember you are from Cork,'
and
'Treat people the way you would like to be treated yourself,'
and also
'Remember your manners.'

Brian Keenan,
Writer and Broadcaster

I remember my mother frequently telling me, 'Be careful what you want, for if you really want it hard enough, you might just get it.'

Sarah Kelleher, Director, Lourdes Youth and Community Services (LYCS)

My mother always says, 'Opportunity knocks just once so take it.'

John Kelly, Writer and Broadcaster

My mother always used to say, 'Fix yourself up: you're like the wreck of the *Hesperus*.'

Enda Kenny TD, Leader, Fine Gael

My mother used to say, 'I've seen it all before.'

Richard Kirwan, Former Director of the Ordnance Survey and Author

Once the tea was finished every evening, my mother used to say, 'Out with the rosary beads and turn off the wireless.'

Seanie Lambe, Community Activist

My mother always used to say, 'You can share a peanut.'

Celia Larkin, Beauty at Blue Door

My mother always used to say, 'Let there be no panic, and if there is let it be organised.'

Also she would say, 'Isn't it great to be alive and so many dead!'

Louis le Brocquy, Visual Artist

My mother, Sybil le Brocquy, used to say, 'Always keep the taxi if you want to arrive at your destination.'

Michael Longley, Poet

When my twin and I quarrelled my parents used to say, 'Little birds in their nest agree.'

When they and their friends were lighting cigarettes my parents used to say, 'Never take the third light,' a superstition from the Great War in which my father fought.

If I was picking my nose my mother would say, 'Bring us down a picture of the Pope.'

Edouard Loubet, Michelin-starred Chef, Bonnieux en Provence

Ma mère a toujours dit, 'Quand on veut, on peut.'
(What you want to do, you can do.)

Joanna Lumley, Actress

My mother often quoted the poet Tagore:

> *Nothing lasts forever, brother – nothing lasts for long*
> *Keep that in your heart and rejoice.*

Michael McDowell SC

My mother always used to say, 'Do what you think is right.'

Finn Mac Eoin, Author

My mother, who is also a published author, used to say, 'I'm always suspicious of a house without books,'
   and
   'Take time and care will ensue.'

Shane McGowan, Singer and Songwriter

My mother, Thérèse, used to say, 'Today's thugs, tomorrow's heroes,'
 and
 'Everybody is shy, at least as shy as you are: remember that.'

Mairead McGuinness MEP

My mother always used to say, 'We'll sit down when we get all the little jobs done,'
  and
  'Get up and help your father.'
  and
  'Get up and don't let anyone see you in bed at this hour of the day.'

Susan McKay, Journalist, Writer and Director of the National Women's Council of Ireland

My mother, Joan McKay, says, 'Give a thing, take a thing is a bad man's play.'

My grandfather, Bob Rodgers, always used to say when someone was staring, 'You're like a hen looking into a bottle.'

Sean McMahon, Writer and Editor

My mother, Peggy, always used to say, 'You'll have to eat a ton of dirt before you die.'

Niall MacMonagle, Writer and Critic

My mother, Lil, always used to say, 'You'd excite a nation.'

Christy Moore,
Singer and Songwriter

My mother, Nancy Power, would say, 'It's not everyone that money suits,'

Her mother, Elly Power, would say (after farting), 'That would melt a foot of snow.'

My other granny, Bridie Dowling, would say, 'That fellow would ate his way to Calvary and back.'

Danny Morrison, Writer

My mother, Susan, was devastated when her mother, my Granny White, died in 1959. I often found her crying when the song 'A Mother's Love's a Blessing' came on the radio.

> *A mother's love's a blessing, no matter where you roam.*
> *Keep her while she's living 'cause you'll miss her when she's gone.*
> *Love her as in childhood, though, feeble, old and grey,*
> *For you'll never miss your mother's love till she's buried beneath the clay.*

Nick Munier, Maître d'Hôtel, *Hell's Kitchen*, and Restaurateur

My mother always used to say, 'Fine food, starch removed,'
and
'If you have a talent never hide it.'

Bryan Murray, Actor, *Fair City*

My mother had a lot of sayings that have stuck with me over the years. I think the one, 'Life is for living, not for throwing away,' is one that gets more potent the older I get.

Bláthnaid Ní Chofaigh, TV presenter

My mother used to say, 'It's a long road that has no turning,'
and
'Blue and green should never be seen unless there is a colour in between.'
This used to drive me and my sisters mad because these two colours are lovely together.

My granny always used to say, 'You would live after seeing her.'

Joy Neville, Captain of the Irish Women's Rugby Team

My mother always used to say, 'You can walk a thousand miles but you can only take one step at a time.'

Pat Nolan, Actor, *Fair City*

My mother always used to say, 'A good run is better than a bad stand.'
   and
   'A robber can hide but a liar can't.'

Miriam O'Callaghan, Broadcaster

My mother always used to say, 'Treat everyone you meet in life well and with respect, and life will almost always look after you.'

Enda O'Coineen,
Yachtsman and Entrepreneur

My mother always used to say, 'If you're bored, it's an insult to yourself.'

Aidan O'Connor,
Journalist and Author

Mom's six boys were all lucky enough to have been schooled and educated at third level. As a child and teenager, I rebelled against almost everything, and I'm sorry now I never really took her wisdom to heart when she used to say, 'Mind your books, boyeen, and your books will mind you.'

Jo O'Donoghue,
Writer and Publisher

My mother, Hanna Buckley, used to say of us seven children, 'Ye'd eat the quarter sessions, judge and all!'

My father, P.J. O'Donoghue, often used to say, 'The more I see of people the more I like my dog.'

Hector Ó hEochagáin, Broadcaster

My mother always used to say, 'When the time is right, the time is right.'

Sharon Osborne, Judge,
American Idol and *The X Factor*

My mother always used to say, 'Be nice to people on the way up, as they will be waiting for you on the way down.'

Maureen O'Sullivan TD, Dublin Central

My mother used to say, 'Know your own country first before you go off travelling to other countries.'

Sir Michael Parkinson, Broadcaster and Author

My father always used to say, 'If I ever see you at the pit gates, I'll kick your backside all the way home.'

Jim Power, Economist and Author

My mother is a total pacifist and would do anything to avoid conflict. Years ago when mealtime debates at home threatened to get too serious she would always recommend, '*Dún do bhéal.*' ('Close your mouth.')

To this day, when I get involved in heated arguments with someone like a public-sector union leader on a TV or radio show she offers me the same advice.

When we got involved in something that we later found too onerous she would dismiss our complaints by saying, 'When one enlists, one has to march.' How true.

Suzanne Power,
Writer and journalist

'The cat can look at the Queen,' my mother used to say to get us to realise that no one was better than us. It is her belief, and my father's, that nothing fits into a six-by-two box but bones and what we can afford to leave behind, so why think someone who has something is anything more than you?

Terry Prone, Director of the Communications Clinic, Dublin

My mother used to say, 'The only fabrics to be worn next to the skin are the natural ones.'

Niall Quinn, Chairman, Sunderland FC

My mother always used to say, 'Nobody can outdo the Lord in generosity.'

Pat Rabbitte TD

My father always used to say, 'Remember your roots and where you came from.'

Mary Raftery, Writer, Broadcaster and Television Producer

My mother, Ita Raftery (née Elmes), always used to say, 'Tús maith, leath na hoibre.' (A good start is half the work.)

Eamon Ryan TD, Minister for Communications, Energy and Natural Resources

My mother, Mary Ryan, (née Cahill), always used to say, 'You can only do your best.' This was hugely influential for me in all circumstances.

Gerry Ryan, Broadcaster

My mother used to say, 'Save your breath to cool your porridge,'
　and
　　'Keep your hand on your ha'penny.'

Michael Ryan,
Presenter, *Nationwide*

My mother used to say, 'Better to pick one can of blackberries than to think of picking ten.'

Trevor Sargent TD

My mother always used to say, 'You'll get more with honey than with vinegar.'

Tom Savage,
Chairman, RTÉ Authority

My mother, Mag Savage, used to say, 'To hell with casting up.'

Martina Scanlan, Actress, *Fair City*

We spent many wonderful sunny Sundays on the beaches in Connemara and this saying of my father – 'All aboard for Oranmore, Shanghai and Galway!'– still conjures up the excitement and anticipation of heading off for sing-songs and sandwiches and lemonade, not knowing which beach we were going to on any given day. There was always the element of mystery and surprise and absolute wonder.

Patricia Scanlan, Author

My mother, Bernadette, always used to give me this good advice:

> *'Love many, trust few, always paddle your own canoe.'*

Ruth Scott, Broadcaster

My mother has this poem on the family fridge:

Rules for a Happy Home

If you get it out - use it
If you sleep on it – make it up.
If you wear it – hang it up
If you drop it – pick it up
If you dirty it – wash it
If you open it – close it
If you turn it on – turn it off
If it rings – answer it
If it needs love – hug and kiss it.

John Spillane,
Singer and Songwriter

My mother always used to say, 'With patience and perseverance you could take a donkey from Kinsale to Jerusalem.'

Kevin Thornton,
Michelin-starred Chef
and Restaurateur

A phrase that was always used by both my parents (my father in particular) was, 'If a job is worth doing it's worth doing well.' I can still hear it being said and it is a phrase which constantly springs to mind. I find myself using it with my children and in a work setting.

Paula Tilbrook,
Actress, *Emmerdale Farm*

'My mother always used to say, 'Nice is as nice does,'
 and
 'Show me your friends and I'll tell you what you are.'

Fergal Tobin, Publishing Director, Gill and Macmillan

My mother used to say, 'Watch your language because it's a precision tool: it's a scalpel, not an axe.'

Ronan Tynan, Tenor

My mother always used to say, 'Dreams are for dreamers, Ronan. Goals are for you and me.'

Marty Whelan, Broadcaster

My mother always used to say, 'Leave your troubles at the bottom of the stairs.'

Marco Pierre White, Head Chef, *Hell's Kitchen*, and Restaurateur

My mother used to say, 'If somebody's not nice to you, be nice to them,' and when I asked why, she said, 'To show them you're a nice person.'

Also she would say, 'A tree without roots is just a piece of wood.'

Victoria White, Author

My mother, Edna White (née McGuckin), an Ulster Protestant born in 1920 amid memories of the Great War, used to say, 'War is a *terrible* thing.'

Xenia, Levis Strauss Model, 1972

My mother always used to say, 'Sitting is bad for your complexion.